SELECTED POEMS OF

DAVID HERBERT LAWRENCE

THE POETRY BOOKSHELF

General Editor: James Reeves

Robert Graves: *English and Scottish Ballads*
Tom Scott: *Late Medieval Scots Poetry*
James Reeves: *Chaucer: Lyric and Allegory*
William Tydeman: *English Poetry 1400–1580*
Martin Seymour-Smith: *Shakespeare's Sonnets*
Martin Seymour-Smith: *Longer Elizabethan Poems*
James Reeves: *John Donne*
Maurice Hussey: *Jonson and the Cavaliers*
Jack Dalglish: *Eight Metaphysical Poets*
James Reeves and Martin Seymour-Smith: *Andrew Marvell*
Gareth Reeves: *George Herbert*
Dennis Burden: *Shorter Poems of John Milton*
V. de S. Pinto: *Poetry of the Restoration*
Roger Sharrock: *John Dryden*
James Reeves: *Jonathan Swift*
John Heath-Stubbs: *Alexander Pope*
Francis Venables: *The Early Augustans*
Donald Davie: *The Late Augustans*
F. W. Bateson: *William Blake*
G. S. Fraser: *Robert Burns*
Roger Sharrock: *William Wordsworth*
James Reeves: *S. T. Coleridge*
Robin Skelton: *Lord Byron*
John Holloway: *P. B. Shelley*
James Reeves: *John Clare*
Robert Gittings: *Poems and Letters of John Keats*
Edmund Blunden: *Alfred Lord Tennyson*
James Reeves: *Robert Browning*
Denys Thompson: *Poetry and Prose of Matthew Arnold*
James Reeves: *Emily Dickinson*
James Reeves: *G. M. Hopkins*
David Wright: *Seven Victorian Poets*
James Reeves: *The Modern Poets' World*
James Reeves: *D. H. Lawrence*

D. H. LAWRENCE
1929

SELECTED POEMS OF
D. H. LAWRENCE

Edited with an Introduction

by

JAMES REEVES

HEINEMANN
LONDON

Heinemann Educational Books Ltd

LONDON EDINBURGH MELBOURNE AUCKLAND TORONTO
SINGAPORE HONG KONG KUALA LUMPUR
IBADAN NAIROBI JOHANNESBURG
LUSAKA NEW DELHI

ISBN 0 435 15000 6 (cased)
ISBN 0 435 15001 4 (paperback)

D. H. LAWRENCE 1885–1930
INTRODUCTION © JAMES REEVES 1967

FIRST PUBLISHED 1951
REPRINTED IN LARGER FORMAT 1958
REPRINTED 1960, 1961, 1963, 1966
THIRD EDITION 1967
REPRINTED 1969, 1970, 1974

Published by
Heinemann Educational Books Ltd
48 Charles Street, London W1X 8AH
Printed in Great Britain by Morrison & Gibb Ltd
London and Edinburgh

CONTENTS

INTRODUCTION

LAWRENCE was not a great poet—if only because poetry was not his main concern as a writer; he was not a good poet in the technical sense. Yet he had touches of greatness, as in a few poems where his dignity as a man transcends the irritation and maladjustment which characterised his normal relations with life. In *Bavarian Gentians*, for instance, he attains to something of the earnestness and composure which seem to go with true greatness. He might have been a good poet had he been less himself. Impatience with poetic technique was, however, a part of him. He had not the craftsman's sense of words as living things, as an end in themselves; words were too much a means to an end. What that end was will be considered.

But Lawrence was an exciting and original poet. If he bores or exasperates, it is seldom because of his subject-matter but usually because of his handling of it. Yet a poet of to-day—especially a young poet—can learn more from the imperfections of Lawrence than from the technical perfection of many better poets. Technical perfection without poetic insight—in short, slickness—is the commonest fault of young poetry to-day. There are not enough young poets prepared to give themselves away by writing badly. Lawrence was always prepared to give himself away, and often wrote badly. It has been my object in making this selection to show Lawrence at his best. I have not included any poems which seem to me wholly bad. There is, however, mixed up with nearly all his good work quite enough bad workmanship to show Lawrence's faults, if not at their worst, at least at their most characteristic.

There has been too much curiosity about Lawrence's life in proportion to the serious critical interest shown in his work. It is enough to say—as might be deduced from even so small a selection as this—that he was a gifted and sensitive child of proletarian parents, and that he was a chronically sick man. With his working-class origin are connected his independence of mind, developing at its worst into a cocky self-assertiveness; his limited traditional education, which forced him to be original but made his judgments often wild and unsystematic; and his originality. He did not derive his experience from books, nor his urge to literary expression from a literary family tradition. He was gifted with acute emotional and physical sensibility, derived perhaps from his refined and sensitive mother, and this drove him naturally to a continuous effort of self-expression. His early work—indeed, all his work—was born out of his acute awareness of physical and emotional experience. With this abnormal sensitiveness is connected also the tubercular malady which afflicted him throughout his forty-five years of life. Like many others so afflicted, he was restless, excitable and at times irritable. His best work, however, especially his early poetry, shows little sign of this irritability; and it is in this work that we see his physical sensibility at its finest. In reading it one has so often the feeling of being in contact with nature at a level just below one's skin. This hypersensitive, as it were subcutaneous, quality in Lawrence's poetry is what makes it exciting, even painful, to read. It gives one the feeling that only the finest descriptive poetry gives—that of seeing things for the first time, and of being in direct sensuous touch with the external world.

Lawrence's principal energy as a writer went into the creation of psychological fiction. As a novelist he was concerned chiefly with the relations between men and women. At his best he represented as no other writer so far had done the conflicts and strains of adolescent growth, the nervous battles just below the surface of emotional and domestic life. There is always strain, conflict, restlessness; his characters live and grow, they are never matured and completed. Lawrence used poetry, as I have suggested, more as a means than as an end. He wrote poems, not as finished creations to be added to the store of English poems, but as a way of expressing his relations with the world. He can seldom have conceived a poem as a whole before he sat down to write it. It grew under his pen. It took on a life of its own, or rather it derived its life from his continuous flow of sensation and impression. Consider, for instance, the poem entitled *End of Another Home Holiday*. Here Lawrence realises vividly the nostalgia, the sense of personal inadequacy, the intense feeling for his mother which characterise much of his writing at this period. The emotion, like so many youthful emotions, was all the more painful for being confused and only semi-articulate. The form of the poem—if it has any form—is organic. It resembles that of a musical impromptu, a series of loosely connected variations. Notice how the poem is first written, then re-written in a more expanded version. Only occasionally does Lawrence seem to be concerned with poetic form as such—in, for instance, *Piano* and *A Youth Mowing*. These poems are different from most of the others in that they are more complete, and more memorable. We find here something of the compression, the economy, the felicity of phrase which we associate with poems we call classical. Lawrence's poetry is not memorable, for all its interest; it is not quotable; it is not, in my opinion, best read aloud. He wrote as it were with the inward eye, not for the outward ear; he writes for the silent reader's inward response.

For the most part, Lawrence's poems were the reverse of classical. What he valued in a thought, as he says in the Foreword to the volume called PANSIES, was its fleeting quality. He wanted these poems to be regarded, not as "immortelles", but as living flowers. His method hovered, to use the jargon of painting, between impressionism and expressionism. He was fascinated by pictures and was himself a painter. One of the poems in this book is the expression of his reactions to the impressionist pictures of Corot. As an impressionist Lawrence was concerned to convey, with the utmost purity possible, his sensations of the external world as it appeared to him at the moment of experience. In *Baby Running Barefoot*, *After the Opera*, *Morning Walk*, and *Coming Awake*, there is an acute realisation of physical impressions based on the purest possible observation. It is in this sense that his poems are valuable for their originality. He shows little "influence", in the accepted sense, but that of Whitman, and in comparison Whitman was a crude observer. If Lawrence's poems had betrayed more of the influence of other writers, his observation could not have been so pure, fresh and true. In *Letter from Town: On a Grey Morning in March* the imagery is throughout rich in clear and vivid impressions. In particular the comparison between the rushing car and the wind conveys just that hint of nostalgia for the country which is intended.

But it was not the limited ends of impressionism at which Lawrence was aiming. This objectivity was quite outside his nature. Even at his most objective, he was never content merely to observe. Just as in his novels he was concerned with the sensations and emotions of his characters, so in his poems he was concerned above all with his own sensations; with the world, that is, not as it might have been to some dispassionate eye, but as it was to *him*, at that particular moment and in that particular state of mind. From this concern arose the faculty of self-projection, of seeing nature not as it was but as it expressed the artist's own moods, which characterises the expressionist, as distinct from the impressionist approach. The distortions of, for instance, Van Gogh in painting arise from the same urge to interpret the visible world in terms of the artist's own temperament which led Lawrence to write such poems as *Weeknight Service* and *Bat*.

The idea of Lawrence as an expressionist poet must be considered more closely. Like Van Gogh, Lawrence was a romantic, with the same restless, dissatisfied, somewhat violent temperament. Both used the external world on which to project their own original natures. Both distorted nature for this purpose. Lawrence's *Mosquito* is no entomologist's specimen. There never was a mosquito quite like it. But how exactly Lawrence realises it as the expression of his intense anger and irritation. The poem is repetitive, wasteful and explosive, like the feelings aroused by the mosquito. One cannot help perceiving the contrast with Donne's *Flea*, in which he makes no attempt to picture the insect, but uses it simply as the occasion of an intricate intellectual speculation. The flea itself is hardly present in the poem except as the starting-point for the argument. But

Lawrence's mosquito is only too maddeningly present. It is a remarkable feature of Lawrence's expressionism that, even when—as in *Kangaroo*—he intellectualises the experience, the occasion of the poem is always physically present, with an acute, sometimes uncomfortable, actuality. *Kangaroo* is, indeed, one of the most completely successful of Lawrence's animal-poems. It expresses a wonderful sensitivity to the physical actuality of the animal. The "philosophy" may or may not be nonsense, but if the kangaroo has a "meaning", surely Lawrence came nearer to realising it than any other writer could have done.

What is the external world which Lawrence experienced so acutely? And what were the sensations which he strove to project upon it? In his early poems the recurrent theme is that of nostalgia for the scenes of his mother-dominated childhood in the Midland countryside where his father worked as a miner. As in most youthful poetry there is much self-pity, much half-articulate adolescent agony, but also a painful and tender delight in the beauty of spring, of flowers, and of early love. Lawrence's imaginative sympathy with the moods and struggles of childhood is profound. *Discord in Childhood* is a terrifyingly successful poem. *Baby Running Barefoot* is one of the few poems on babyhood which show absolutely no trace of sentimentality. In *Snapdragon* (a sort of psychological short story in verse) and the poems of the Bavarian and Italian period, he has overcome the adolescent introspectiveness of the earlier period and has begun to feel his way into the emotional lives of others, such as German and Italian peasants. He had begun to diagnose the malady of civilised, urban society—particularly that of the middle class into which his literary aspirations had projected him—in terms of his own lack of balance between mental experience and physical fulfilment. He came to distrust mind as the agency by which civilisation had torn men from their roots in bodily well-being and the awareness of physical life. Men's psychological balance was destroyed by the strains placed upon them through the necessity of following the artificial routine of urban convention; the machine had destroyed man's dignity and taken away from him the joy of creative work with his hands; if man tried to live separated from the forces that bind him to nature and the origins of his own being, he became nervously exhausted, fretful and dissatisfied. This is the theme of many of the poems in PANSIES. It is, of course, a commonplace of much romantic thought from Rousseau onwards. But Lawrence was the most striking protagonist of the natural man since the maturity of industrialism. Much of his life, therefore, was spent in search not only of bodily and spiritual health for himself, but of whatever traces still remained of the perfect "natural" society which was postulated by all romantic idealists. London and the English Midlands, Bavaria, Sicily, Australia, Mexico—the search led Lawrence across the world, and in this book are poems written in all these places. There is in many of the poems a lively vein of social criticism. In the half-dozen poems beginning with *A Living*, Lawrence appears directly as a moralist; and in the passage from *Hibiscus and Salvia Flowers* he expresses detestation of modern egalitarian socialism and a longing for the lost dignity of royalty. This thought recurs in *Snake*, where he recounts with wearied self-disgust how his "accursed human education" made him dishonour a creature who appeared like a lost king of the underworld.

The peasants of Italy and Bavaria he found to be in reality not much less removed from the fundamental natural life than were the schoolboys of Croydon or the shop-girls of the industrial Midlands. So his eager desire for communion with natural forces led him to an imaginative study of birds, beasts and flowers. From this were produced his mature poems of self-projection. The circus-elephant, the bat, the tortoise, the kangaroo, the humming-bird, the blue jay—all seemed to Lawrence living evidence of a primordial, instinctive existence in which man had once participated but from which he was now, to his destruction, cut off.

This return, in spirit, to an animal world, as a relief from, and a solution to, the despair which civilisation produced, suggests a tragic view of life—a view which was the result of Lawrence's own life, in a sense tragic, despite the measure of self-fulfilment which he achieved. Lawrence is always written of as a gay companion, and

6

there is in his poems much gaiety, though it is often drowned by a note of shrill expostulation against the stupidity of society and the interference of policemen with his writings and paintings. There is a small volume, called NETTLES, poetically so bad that I have not been able to include even one example. It is nothing but a self-righteous scream of exasperation against authority. In his fight with the censorship Lawrence, sick as he was, was amply justified in his exasperation and petulance, but it would have been more poetic not to have published his exasperation so stridently.

Tragic as was Lawrence's view of civilisation, there is always sufficient truth in the warning against mechanisation, industrialism and intellect for it to have recurrent significance at least as a corrective. That Lawrence's thought has had immense influence is proof that many are aware of the danger of separating life too completely from its physical roots. Wordsworth had realised that the springs of our nature lie deeper than convention, and in retreating from the implications of his discovery he stultified himself as a poet during the latter half of his life. Lawrence never flinched from his search, and in following it he wore himself out.

Even though Lawrence did not devote his main creative energy to writing poems, he lived the life of a poet. The extraordinary sensitiveness to impressions and his extraordinary command of imagery in which to express it never failed him. In his later poems there is no diminution of nervous sensibility; there is even an increase in dignity, seriousness and the suggestion of hidden sources of evocation. Lawrence relied less than nearly all other poets on the established symbolism of the past. In the volume called LAST POEMS, from which *The Argonauts*, *They Say the Sea is Loveless*, *Bavarian Gentians* and *The Ship of Death* are taken, there appears a realisation of the beauty of classical myth. But just as Lawrence had never looked at an express train, a London suburb or a wild bird with the eyes of another poet, so in *Bavarian Gentians*, one of his most impressive and beautiful poems he gave his own interpretation to the perennial myth of Persephone. And in the mysterious and moving *Ship of Death* he turns his oldest and most persistent fault, that of

7

repetitiveness, into a virtue, for here the repetition becomes a ritual incantation suggesting the solemnity of his own approaching end.

I have tried to show how Lawrence's thought was bound up with his life and how his poems were connected with his thought. Life, thought and poems make—with the novels and other writings—a unity more clearly exemplified, without irrelevant deviation, than is the case with any other writer of modern times. Why Lawrence was not wholly and successfully a poet is too big a question to consider here. It is bound up with the difficult question of *form* in the poems. For the form of a poem *is* the poem; and the more a writer appears to despise form, or to be impatient with it, the more he evades the problem of how to be a poet. In so far as Lawrence was not a poet, it was because he was not interested in poetic form, or failed to evolve new forms. His repetitiveness has been commented on. There are poems which any competent craftsman could "improve" by condensation. It may be asked why Lawrence did not do this himself. It seems as if he was afraid of alteration, afraid that his poems would lose spontaneity and something of the life which they drew from him as he wrote them. Many of them are straggling notebook pieces without design or conclusion. Many are almost "automatic". In searching for a word to convey an impression, or hit off a mood, he stumbles on one which he finds felicitous and is sidetracked from his theme, repeating the word again and again, as if to reinforce the impression by sheer willpower. As often as not, the impulse is not reinforced but dissipated and the poem sprawls in pieces on the page. This effect is heightened by Lawrence's use of a slack, conversational rhythm. This rhythm is of course inseparable from Lawrence's method of expression. In his best poems the rhythm is absolutely right for the feeling and mood he wishes to communicate. How perfectly, for instance, is the authenticity of the experience in *Snake* rendered in the conversational, informal rhythm. How perfectly the nervous, unequal, jerky lines of *Bat* express the bat's flight and the writer's uneasy discomfort. Lawrence's free rhythm is characteristic. But it is a rhythm which can only reinforce the effect of formlessness. Since

8

Chaucer established the supremacy of iambic metres over the native alliterative verse, no poet has successfully deviated for long from the iambic norm. Even a considerable achievement like the poems of Whitman seems rough, shapeless and somehow provincial. To go further, however, would be to make the mistake of writing of Lawrence as if he could have been otherwise than he was. If he was not a poet in any traditional sense, it was because he was not interested in being one. What we have is not a body of formally memorable and satisfying poems, but the almost unshaped utterance of a keen and vital poetic sensibility, valuing the expression of feeling and mood, rebelling against discipline and control.

Note to the Third Edition

In this edition I have added a further thirty-three poems to the original selection, and also an Index of first lines and a Bibliography.

J. R.
1967

SELECT BIBLIOGRAPHY

STANDARD EDITION

The Complete Poems, ed. Vivian de Sola Pinto and Warren Roberts, 2 vols. (Heinemann, 1964).

RELEVANT TEXTS

Collected Letters, ed. Harry T. Moore, 2 vols. (Heinemann, 1962).

Letters, ed. Aldous Huxley (Heinemann, 1932).

D. H. Lawrence: Selected Literary Criticism, ed. Anthony Beal (Heinemann, 1956, paperback, 1961).

D. H. Lawrence, *Mornings in Mexico* and *Etruscan Palaces* (Heinemann, Phoenix Edition, 1956).

D. H. Lawrence, *Sea and Sardinia* (Heinemann, Phoenix Edition, 1956).

D. H. Lawrence, *Twilight in Italy* (Heinemann, Phoenix Edition, 1956).

BIOGRAPHY AND CRITICISM

A D. H. Lawrence Miscellany, ed. Harry T. Moore (Heinemann, 1961).

Harry T. Moore, *The Life and Works of D. H. Lawrence* (Allen & Unwin, 1951).

Harry T. Moore and Warren Roberts, *D. H. Lawrence and his World* (Thames & Hudson, Pictorial Biographies Series, 1966).

Keith Sagar, *The Art of D. H. Lawrence* (Cambridge University Press, 1966).

Anthony West, *D. H. Lawrence* (Arthur Barker, European Novelists Series, 1966).

Anthony Beal, *D. H. Lawrence* (Oliver & Boyd, Writers & Critics Series, 1961).

Kenneth Young, *D. H. Lawrence* (British Council: Longmans, Writers and Their Works Series, 1952).

Graham Hough, *Two Exiles: Lord Byron and D. H. Lawrence* (Lecture at the University of Nottingham, 1956).

Dog-Tired

If she would come to me here
    Now the sunken swaths
    Are glittering paths
To the sun, and the swallows cut clear
Into the setting sun! if she came to me here!

If she would come to me now,
Before the last-mown harebells are dead;
While that vetch-clump still burns red!
Before all the bats have dropped from the bough
To cool in the night; if she came to me now!

The horses are untackled, the chattering machine
Is still at last. If she would come
We could gather up the dry hay from
The hill-brow, and lie quite still, till the green
Sky ceased to quiver, and lost its active sheen.

I should like to drop
On the hay, with my head on her knee,
And lie dead still, while she
Breathed quiet above me; and the crop
Of stars grew silently.

I should like to lie still
As if I was dead; but feeling
Her hand go stealing
Over my face and my head, until
This ache was shed.

Discord in Childhood

Outside the house an ash-tree hung its terrible whips,
And at night when the wind rose, the lash of the tree
Shrieked and slashed the wind, as a ship's
Weird rigging in a storm shrieks hideously.

Within the house two voices arose, a slender lash
Whistling she-delirious rage, and the dreadful sound
Of a male thong booming and bruising, until it had drowned
The other voice in a silence of blood, 'neath the noise of the ash.

Cherry Robbers

Under the long dark boughs, like jewels red
    In the hair of an Eastern girl
Hang strings of crimson cherries, as if had bled
    Blood-drops beneath each curl.

Under the glistening cherries, with folded wings
    Three dead birds lie:
Pale-breasted throstles and a blackbird, robberlings
    Stained with red dye.

Against the haystack a girl stands laughing at me,
    Cherries hung round her ears.
Offers me her scarlet fruit: I will see
    If she has any tears.

Virgin Youth

Now and again
The life that looks through my eyes
And quivers in words through my mouth,
And behaves like the rest of men,
Slips away, so I gasp in surprise.

And then
My unknown breasts begin
To wake, and down the thin
Ripples below the breast an urgent
Rhythm starts, and my silent and slumberous belly
In one moment rouses insurgent.

My soft, slumbering belly,
Quivering awake with one impulse and one will,
Then willy nilly
A lower me gets up and greets me;
Homunculus stirs from his roots, and strives until,
Risen up, he beats me.

He stands, and I tremble before him.
—Who then art thou?—
He is wordless, but sultry and vast,
And I can't deplore him.
—Who art thou? What hast
Thou to do with me, thou lustrous one, iconoclast?—

How beautiful he is! without sound,
Without eyes, without hands;
Yet, flame of the living ground
He stands, the column of fire by night.
And he knows from the depths; he quite
Alone understands.

Quite alone, he alone
Understands and knows.
Lustrously sure, unknown
Out of nowhere he rose.

I tremble in his shadow, as he burns
For the dark goal.
He stands like a lighthouse, night churns
Round his base, his dark light rolls
Into darkness, and darkly returns.

Is he calling, the lone one? Is his deep
Silence full of summons?
Is he moving invisibly? Does his steep
Curve sweep towards a woman's?

Traveller, column of fire,
It is vain.
The glow of thy full desire
Becomes pain.

Dark, ruddy pillar, forgive me! I
Am helplessly bound
To the rock of virginity. Thy
Strange voice has no sound.

We cry in the wilderness. Forgive me, I
Would so gladly lie
In the womanly valley, and ply
Thy twofold dance.

Thou dark one, thou proud, curved beauty! I
Would worship thee, letting my buttocks prance.
But the hosts of men with one voice deny
Me the chance.

They have taken the gates from the hinges
And built up the way. I salute thee
But to deflower thee. Thy tower impinges
On nothingness. Pardon me!

Monologue of a Mother

This is the last of all, then, this is the last!
I must fold my hands, and turn my face to the fire,
And watch my dead days fusing together in dross,
Shape after shape, and scene after scene of my past
Clotting to one dead mass in the sinking fire
Where ash on the dying coals grows swiftly, like heavy moss.

Strange he is, my son, for whom I have waited like a lover;
Strange to me, like a captive in a foreign country, haunting
The confines, gazing out beyond, where the winds go free;
White and gaunt, with wistful eyes that hover
Always on the distance, as if his soul were chaunting
A monotonous weird of departure away from me.

Like a thin white bird blown out of the northern seas,
Like a bird from the far north blown with a broken wing
Into our sooty garden, he drags and beats
Along the fence perpetually, seeking release
From me, from the hand of my love which creeps up, needing
His happiness, whilst he in displeasure retreats.

I must look away from him, for my faded eyes
Like a cringing dog at his heels offend him now,
Like a toothless hound pursuing him with my will;
Till he chafes at my crouching persistence, and a sharp spark flies
In my soul from under the sudden frown of his brow
As he blenches and turns away, and my heart stands still.

This is the last, it will not be any more.
All my life I have borne the burden of myself,
All the long years of sitting in my husband's house;
Never have I said to myself as he closed the door:
"Now I am caught! You are hopelessly lost, O Self!
You are frightened with joy, my heart, like a frightened mouse."

Three times have I offered myself, three times rejected.
It will not be any more. No more, my son, my son!—
Never to know the glad freedom of obedience, since long ago
The angel of childhood kissed me and went! I expected
This last one to claim me;—and now, my son, O my son,
I must sit alone and wait, and never know
The loss of myself, till death comes, who cannot fail.

Death, in whose service is nothing of gladness, takes me;
For the lips and the eyes of God are behind a veil.
And the thought of the lipless voice of the Father shakes me
With dread, and fills my heart with the tears of desire,
And my heart rebels with anguish, as night draws nigher.

The Little Town at Evening

The chime of the bells, and the church clock striking eight
Solemnly and distinctly cries down the babel of children still
    playing in the hay.
The church draws nearer upon us, gentle and great
In shadow, covering us up with her grey.

Like drowsy creatures, the houses fall asleep
Under the fleece of shadow, as in between
Tall and dark the church moves, anxious to keep
Their sleeping, cover them soft unseen.

Hardly a murmur comes from the sleeping brood;
I wish the church had covered me up with the rest
In the home-place. Why is it she should exclude
Me so distinctly from sleeping the sleep I'd love best?

Last Hours

The cool of an oak's unchequered shade
Falls on me as I lie in deep grass
Which rushes upward, blade beyond blade.
While higher the darting grass-flowers pass
Piercing the blue with their crocketed spires
And waving flags, and the ragged fires
Of the sorrel's cresset—a green, brave town
Vegetable, new in renown.

Over the tree's edge, as over a mountain
Surges the white of the moon,
A cloud comes up like the surge of a fountain,
Pressing round and low at first, but soon
Heaving and piling a round white dome.
How lovely it is to be at home
Like an insect in the grass
Letting life pass!

There s a scent of clover crept through my hair
From the full resource of some purple dome
Where that lumbering bee, who can hardly bear
His burden above me, never has clomb.
But not even the scent of insouciant flowers
Makes pause the hours.

Down the valley roars a townward train.
I hear it through the grass
Dragging the links of my shortening chain
Southwards, alas!

Weeknight Service

The five old bells
Are hurrying and stridently calling,
Insisting, protesting
They are right, yet clamorously falling
Into gabbling confusion, without resting,
Like spattering shouts of an orator endlessly dropping
From the tower on the town, but endlessly, never stopping.

The silver moon
That somebody has spun so high
To settle the question, heads or tails? has caught
In the net of the night's balloon,
And sits with a smooth, bland smile up there in the sky
Serenely smiling at naught,
Unless the little star that keeps her company
Makes tittering jests at the bells' obscenity;
As if *he* knew aught!

While patient Night
Sits indifferent, hugged in her rags;
She neither knows nor cares
Why the old church bellows and brags;
The noise distresses her ears, and tears
At her tattered silence, as she crouches and covers her face
Bent, if we did but know it, on a weary and bitter grimace.

18

The wise old trees
Drop their leaves with a faint, sharp hiss of contempt;
A car at the end of the street goes by with a laugh.
As by degrees
The damned bells cease, and we are exempt,
And the stars can chaff
The cool high moon at their ease; while the droning church
Is peopled with shadows and wailing, and last ghosts lurch
Towards its cenotaph.

Letter from Town: On a Grey Morning in March

The clouds are pushing in grey reluctance slowly northward to you,
    While north of them all, at the farthest ends, stands one bright-
    bosomed, aglance
With fire as it guards the wild north-coasts, red-fire seas running
through
    The rocks where ravens flying to windward melt as a well-shot
    lance.

You should be out by the orchard, where violets secretly darken
the earth,
    Or there in the woods of the twilight, with northern wind-flowers
    shaken astir.
Think of me here in the library, trying and trying a song that is
worth
    Tears and swords to my heart, arrows no armour will turn or
    deter.

You tell me the lambs have come, they lie like daisies white in
the grass
    Of the dark-green hills; new calves in shed; peewits turn after
    the plough—

It is well for you. For me the navvies work in the road where I pass
  And I want to smite in anger the barren rock of each waterless
    brow.

Like the sough of a wind that is caught up high in the mesh of the
    budding trees,
  A sudden car goes sweeping past, and I strain my soul to hear
The voice of the furtive triumphant engine as it rushes past like a
    breeze,
    To hear on its mocking triumphance unwitting the after-echo
    of fear.

Letter from Town: The Almond-Tree

You promised to send me some violets. Did you forget?
  White ones and blue ones from under the orchard hedge?
  Sweet dark purple, and white ones mixed for a pledge
Of our early love that hardly has opened yet.

Here there's an almond-tree—you have never seen
  Such a one in the north—it flowers on the street, and I stand
  Every day by the fence to look up at the flowers that expand
At rest in the blue, and wonder at what they mean.

Under the almond-tree, the happy lands
  Provence, Japan, and Italy repose;
  And passing feet are chatter and clapping of those
Who play around us, country girls clapping their hands.

You, my love, the foremost, in a flowered gown,
  All your unbearable tenderness, you with the laughter
  Startled upon your eyes now so wide with hereafter,
You with loose hands of abandonment hanging down.

End of Another Home Holiday

When shall I see the half-moon sink again
Behind the black sycamore at the end of the garden?
When will the scent of the dim white phlox
Creep up the wall to me, and in at my open window?

Why is it, the long, slow stroke of the midnight bell
      (Will it never finish the twelve?)
Falls again and again on my heart with a heavy reproach?
The moon-mist is over the village, out of the mist speaks the bell,
And all the little roofs of the village bow low, pitiful, beseeching,
    resigned.
—Speak, you my home! what is it I don't do well?

Ah home, suddenly I love you
As I hear the sharp clean trot of a pony down the road,
Succeeding sharp little sounds dropping into silence
Clear upon the long-drawn hoarseness of a train across the valley.

.   .   .   .   .   .

The light has gone out, from under my mother's door.
    That she should love me so!—
    She, so lonely, greying now!
    And I leaving her,
    Bent on my pursuits!

      Love is the great Asker.
      The sun and the rain do not ask the secret
      Of the time when the grain struggles down in the dark.
      The moon walks her lonely way without anguish,
      Because no one grieves over her departure.

Forever, ever by my shoulder pitiful love will linger,
Crouching as little houses crouch under the mist when I turn.
Forever, out of the mist, the church lifts up a reproachful finger,
Pointing my eyes in wretched defiance where love hides her face
　　to mourn.

> Oh! but the rain creeps down to wet the grain
> That struggles alone in the dark,
> And asking nothing, patiently steals back again!
> The moon sets forth o' nights
> To walk the lonely, dusky heights
> Serenely, with steps unswerving;
> Pursued by no sigh of bereavement,
> No tears of love unnerving
> Her constant tread:
> While ever at my side,
> Frail and sad, with grey, bowed head,
> The beggar-woman, the yearning-eyed
> Inexorable love goes lagging.

The wild young heifer, glancing distraught,
With a strange new knocking of life at her side
　　Runs seeking a loneliness.
The little grain draws down the earth, to hide
Nay, even the slumberous egg, as it labours under the shell
　　Patiently to divide and self-divide,
Asks to be hidden, and wishes nothing to tell.

But when I draw the scanty cloak of silence over my eyes
Piteous love comes peering under the hood;
Touches the clasp with trembling fingers, and tries
To put her ears to the painful sob of my blood;
While her tears soak through to my breast,
　　Where they burn and cauterise.

.　　.　　.　　.　　.　　.

The moon lies back and reddens.
In the valley a corncrake calls
    Monotonously,
With a plaintive, unalterable voice, that deadens
    My confident activity;
With a horse, insistent request that falls
    Unweariedly, unweariedly,
      Asking something more of me,
        Yet more of me.

Baby Running Barefoot

When the white feet of the baby beat across the grass
The little white feet nod like white flowers in a wind,
They poise and run like puffs of wind that pass
Over water where the weeds are thinned.

And the sight of their white playing in the grass
Is winsome as a robin's song, so fluttering;
Or like two butterflies that settle on a glass
Cup for a moment, soft little wing-beats uttering.

And I wish that the baby would tack across here to me
Like a wind-shadow running on a pond, so she could stand
With two little bare white feet upon my knee
And I could feel her feet in either hand

Cool as syringa buds in morning hours,
Or firm and silken as young peony flowers.

Aware

Slowly the moon is rising out of the ruddy haze,
Divesting herself of her golden shift, and so
Emerging white and exquisite; and I in amaze
See in the sky before me, a woman I did not know
I loved, but there she goes, and her beauty hurts my heart;
I follow her down the night, begging her not to depart.

A White Blossom

A tiny moon as small and white as a single jasmine flower
Leans all alone above my window, on night's wintry bower,
Liquid as lime-tree blossom, soft as brilliant water or rain
She shines, the first white love of my youth, passionless and in vain.

Corot

The trees rise taller and taller, lifted
On a subtle rush of cool grey flame
That issuing out of the east has sifted
    The spirit from each leaf's frame.

For the trailing, leisurely rapture of life
Drifts dimly forward, easily hidden
By bright leaves uttered aloud; and strife
    Of shapes by a hard wind ridden.

The grey, plasm-limpid, pellucid advance
Of the luminous purpose of Life shines out
Where lofty trees athwart-stream chance
    To shake flakes of its shadow about.

The subtle, steady rush of the whole
Grey foam-mist of advancing Time
As it silently sweeps to its somewhere, its goal,
    Is seen in the gossamer's rime.

Is heard in the windless whisper of leaves,
In the silent labours of men in the field,
In the downward-dropping of flimsy sheaves
    Of cloud the rain-skies yield.

In the tapping haste of a fallen leaf,
In the flapping of red-roof smoke, and the small
Footstepping tap of men beneath
    Dim trees so huge and tall.

For what can all sharp-rimmed substance but catch
In a backward ripple, the wave-length, reveal
For a moment the mighty direction, snatch
    A spark beneath the wheel!

Since Life sweeps whirling, dim and vast,
Creating the channelled vein of man
And leaf for its passage; a shadow cast
    And gone before we can scan.

Ah listen, for silence is not lonely!
Imitate the magnificent trees
That speak no word of their rapture, but only
    Breathe largely the luminous breeze.

After the Opera

Down the stone stairs
Girls with their large eyes wide with tragedy
Lift looks of shocked and momentous emotion up at me.
And I smile.

Ladies
Stepping like birds with their bright and pointed feet
Peer anxiously forth, as if for a boat to carry them out of the
    wreckage;
And among the wreck of the theatre crowd
I stand and smile.
They take tragedy so becomingly;
Which pleases me.

But when I meet the weary eyes
The reddened, aching eyes of the bar-man with thin arms,
I am glad to go back to where I came from.

Morning Work

A gang of labourers on the piled wet timber
That shines blood-red beside the railway siding
Seem to be making out of the blue of the morning
Something faery and fine, the shuttles sliding,

The red-gold spools of their hands and their faces swinging
Hither and thither across the high crystalline frame
Of day: trolls at the cave of ringing cerulean mining
And laughing with labour, living their work like a game.

26

Last Lesson of the Afternoon

When will the bell ring, and end this weariness?
How long have they tugged the leash, and strained apart,
My pack of unruly hounds! I cannot start
Them again on a quarry of knowledge they hate to hunt,
I can haul them and urge them no more.

No longer now can I endure the brunt
Of the books that lie out on the desks; a full threescore
Of several insults of blotted pages, and scrawl
Of slovenly work that they have offered me.
I am sick, and what on earth is the good of it all?
What good to them or me, I cannot see!

                              So, shall I take
My last dear fuel of life to heap on my soul
And kindle my will to a flame that shall consume
Their dross of indifference; and take the toll
Of their insults in punishment?—I will not!—

I will not waste my soul and my strength for this.
What do I care for all that they do amiss!
What is the point of this teaching of mine, and of this
Learning of theirs? It all goes down the same abyss.

What does it matter to me, if they can write
A description of a dog, or if they can't?
What is the point? To us both, it is all my aunt!
And yet I'm supposed to care, with all my might.

I do not, and will not; they won't and they don't; and that's all!
I shall keep my strength for myself; they can keep theirs as well.
Why should we beat our heads against the wall
Of each other? I shall sit and wait for the bell.

A Snowy Day in School

All the long school-hours, round the irregular hum of the class
Have pressed immeasurable spaces of hoarse silence
Muffling my mind, as snow muffles the sounds that pass
Down the soiled street. We have pattered the lessons ceaselessly—

But the faces of the boys, in the brooding, yellow light
Have been for me like a dazed constellation of stars,
Like half-blown flowers dimly shaking at the night,
Like half-seen froth on an ebbing shore in the moon.

Out of each face, strange, dark beams that disquiet;
In the open depths of each flower, dark, restless drops;
Twin-bubbling challenge and mystery, in the foam's whispering
    riot.
—How can I answer the challenge of so many eyes?

The thick snow is crumpled on the roof, it plunges down
Awfully!—Must I call back a hundred eyes?—A voice
Falters a statement about an abstract noun—
What was my question?—My God, must I break this hoarse

Silence that rustles beyond the stars?—There!—
I have startled a hundred eyes, and now I must look
Them an answer back; it is more than I can bear.

The snow descends as if the slow sky shook
In flakes of shadow down; while through the gap
Between the schools sweeps one black rook.

In the playground, a shaggy snowball stands huge and still
With fair flakes lighting down on it. Beyond, the town
Is lost in this shadowed silence the skies distil.

And all things are in silence, they can brood
Alone within the dim and hoarse silence.
Only I and the class must wrangle; this work is a bitter rood!

A Winter's Tale

Yesterday the fields were only grey with scattered snow,
And now the longest grass-leaves hardly emerge;
Yet her deep footsteps mark the snow, and go
On towards the pines at the hill's white verge.

I cannot see her, since the mist's pale scarf
Obscures the dark wood and the dull orange sky;
But she's waiting, I know, impatient and cold, half
Sobs struggling into her frosty sigh.

Why does she come so promptly, when she must know
She's only the nearer to the inevitable farewell?
The hill is steep, on the snow my steps are slow—
Why does she come, when she knows what I have to tell?

Sorrow

Why does the thin grey strand
Floating up from the forgotten
Cigarette between my fingers,
Why does it trouble me?

Ah, you will understand;
When I carried my mother downstairs,
A few times only, at the beginning
Of her soft-foot malady.

I should find, for a reprimand
To my gaiety, a few long grey hairs
On the breast of my coat; and one by one
I watched them float up the dark chimney.

Brooding Grief

A yellow leaf, from the darkness
Hops like a frog before me;
Why should I start and stand still?

I was watching the woman that bore me
Stretched in the brindled darkness
Of the sick-room, rigid with will
To die: and the quick leaf tore me
Back to this rainy swill
Of leaves and lamps and the city street mingled before me.

Snap-Dragon

She made me follow to her garden, where
The mellow sunlight stood as in a cup
Between the old grey walls; I did not dare
To raise my face, I did not dare look up,
Lest her bright eyes like sparrows should fly in
My windows of discovery, and shrill "Sin!"

So with a downcast mien and laughing voice
I followed, followed the swing of her white dress
That rocked in a lilt along; I watched the poise
Of her feet as they flew for a space, then paused to press
The grass deep down with the royal burden of her;
And gladly I'd offered my breast to the tread of her.

"I like to see," she said, and she crouched her down,
She sunk into my sight like a settling bird;
And her bosom couched in the confines of her gown
Like heavy birds at rest there, softly stirred
By her measured breaths: "I like to see," said she,
"The snap-dragon put out his tongue at me."

She laughed, she reached her hand out to the flower,
Closing its crimson throat. My own throat in her power
Strangled, my heart swelled up so full
As if it would burst its wine-skin in my throat,
Choke me in my own crimson. I watched her pull
The gorge of the gaping flower, till the blood did float

Over my eyes, and I was blind—
Her large brown hand stretched over
The windows of my mind;
And there in the dark I did discover
Things I was out to find:

My Grail, a brown bowl twined
With swollen veins that met in the wrist,
Under whose brown the amethyst
I longed to taste! I longed to turn
My heart's red measure in her cup;
I longed to feel my hot blood burn
With the amethyst in her cup.

Then suddenly she looked up,
And I was blind in a tawny-gold day,
Till she took her eyes away.

So she came down from above
And emptied my heart of love.
So I held my heart aloft
To the cuckoo that hung like a dove,
And she settled soft.

It seemed that I and the morning world
Were pressed cup-shape to take this reiver
Bird who was weary to have furled
Her wings in us,
As we were weary to receive her.

>   *This bird, this rich,*
>   *Sumptuous central grain;*
>   *This mutable witch,*
>   *This one refrain,*
>   *This laugh in the fight,*
>   *This clot of night,*
>   *This field of delight.*

She spoke, and I closed my eyes
To shut hallucinations out.
I echoed with surprise
Hearing my mere lips shout
The answer they did devise.

>   Again I saw a brown bird hover
>   Over the flowers at my feet;
>   I felt a brown bird hover
>   Over my heart, and sweet
>   Its shadow lay on my heart.
>   I thought I saw on the clover
>   A brown bee pulling apart
>   The closed flesh of the clover
>   And burrowing in its heart.

>   She moved her hand, and again
>   I felt the brown bird cover
>   My heart; and then
>   The bird came down on my heart,
>   As on a nest the rover
>   Cuckoo comes, and shoves over

The brim each careful part
Of love, takes possession, and settles her down,
With her wings and her feathers to drown
The nest in a heart of love.

She turned her flushed face to me for the glint
Of a moment.—"See," she laughed, "if you also
Can make them yawn!"—I put my hand to the dint
In the flower's throat, and the flower gaped wide with woe.
She watched, she went of a sudden intensely still,
She watched my hand, to see what it would fulfil.

I pressed the wretched, throttled flower between
My fingers, till its head lay back, its fangs
Poised at her. Like a weapon my hand was white and keen,
And I held the choked flower-serpent in its pangs
Of mordant anguish, till she ceased to laugh,
Until her pride's flag, smitten, cleaved down to the staff.

She hid her face, she murmured between her lips
The low word "Don't!"—I let the flower fall,
But held my hand afloat towards the slips
Of blossom she fingered, and my fingers all
Put forth to her: she did not move, nor I,
For my hand like a snake watched hers, that could not fly.

Then I laughed in the dark of my heart, I did exult
Like a sudden chuckling of music. I bade her eyes
Meet mine, I opened her helpless eyes to consult
Their fear, their shame, their joy that underlies
Defeat in such a battle. In the dark of her eyes
My heart was fierce to make her laughter rise.

Till her dark deeps shook with convulsive thrills, and the dark
Of her spirit wavered like watered thrilled with light:

And my heart leaped up in longing to plunge its stark
Fervour within the pool of her twilight,
Within her spacious soul, to find delight.

And I do not care, though the large hands of revenge
Shall get my throat at last, shall get it soon,
If the joy that they are lifted to avenge
Have risen red on my night as a harvest moon,
Which even death can only put out for me;
And death, I know, is better than not-to-be.

Firelight and Nightfall

The darkness steals the forms of all the queens,
But oh, the palms of his two black hands are red
Inflamed with binding up the sheaves of the dead
Hours that were once all glory and all queens.

And I remember still the sunny hours
Of queens in hyacinth and skies of gold,
And morning singing where the woods are scrolled
And diapered above the chaunting flowers.

Here lamps are white like snowdrops in the grass:
The town is like a churchyard, all so still
And grey now night is here; nor will
Another torn red sunset come to pass.

A Passing-Bell

Mournfully to and fro, to and fro the trees are waving,
 What did you say, my dear?
The rain-bruised leaves are suddenly shaken, as a child
Asleep still shakes in the clutch of a sob—
 Yes, my love, I hear.

One lonely bell, one only, the storm-tossed afternoon is braving,
 Why not let it ring?
The roses lean down when they hear it, the tender, mild
Flowers of the bleeding-heart fall to the throb—
 'Tis a little thing!

A wet bird walks on the lawn, call to the boy to come and look,
 Yes, it is over now.
Call to him out of the silence, call him to see
The starling shaking its head as it walks in the grass——
 Ah, who knows how?

He cannot see it, I can never show it him, how it shook
 Don't disturb it, darling!—
Its head as it walked: I can never call him to me,
Never, he *is* not, whatever shall come to pass.
 No, look at the wet starling!

Piano

Softly, in the dusk, a woman is singing to me;
Taking me back down the vista of years, till I see
A child sitting under the piano, in the boom of the tingling strings
And pressing the small, poised feet of a mother who smiles as she
 sings.

35

In spite of myself, the insidious mastery of song
Betrays me back, till the heart of me weeps to belong
To the old Sunday evenings at home, with winter outside
And hymns in the cosy parlour, the tinkling piano our guide.

So now it is vain for the singer to burst into clamour
With the great black piano appassionato. The glamour
Of childish days is upon me, my manhood is cast
Down in the flood of remembrance, I weep like a child for the past.

On the Balcony

In front of the sombre mountains, a faint, lost ribbon of rainbow;
And between us and it, the thunder;
And down below in the green wheat, the labourers
Stand like dark stumps, still in the green wheat.

You are near to me, and your naked feet in their sandals,
And through the scent of the balcony's naked timber
I distinguish the scent of your hair: so now the limber
Lightning falls from heaven.

Adown the pale-green glacier river floats
A dark boat through the gloom—and whither?
The thunder roars. But still we have each other!
The naked lightnings in the heavens dither
And disappear—what have we but each other?
The boat has gone.

Icking.

A Youth Mowing

There are four men mowing down by the Isar;
I can hear the swish of the scythe-strokes, four
Sharp breaths taken: yea, and I
Am sorry for what's in store.

The first man out of the four that's mowing
Is mine, I claim him once and for all;
Though it's sorry I am, on his young feet, knowing
None of the trouble he's led to stall.

As he sees me bringing the dinner, he lifts
His head as proud as a deer that looks
Shoulder-deep out of the corn; and wipes
His scythe-blade bright, unhooks

The scythe-stone and over the stubble to me.
Lad, thou hast gotten a child in me,
Laddie, a man thou'lt ha'e to be,
Yea, though I'm sorry for thee.

A Doe at Evening

As I went through the marshes
a doe sprang out of the corn
and flashed up the hill-side
leaving her fawn.

On the sky-line
she moved round to watch,
she pricked a fine black blotch
on the sky.

I looked at her
and felt her watching;
I became a strange being.
Still, I had my right to be there with her.

Her nimble shadow trotting
along the sky-line, she
put back her fine, level-balanced head.
And I knew her.

Ah yes, being male, is not my head hard-balanced, antlered?
Are not my haunches light?
Has she not fled on the same wind with me?
Does not my fear cover her fear?

Irschenhausen.

Sunday Afternoon in Italy

The man and the maid go side by side
With an interval of space between;
And his hands are awkward and want to hide,
She braves it out since she must be seen.

When some one passes he drops his head,
Shading his face in his black felt hat.
While the hard girl hardens; nothing is said,
There is nothing to wonder or cavil at.

Alone on the open road again,
Wish the mountain snows across the lake
Flushing the afternoon, they are uncomfortable,
The loneliness daunts them, their stiff throats ache.

And he sighs with relief when she parts from him;
Her proud head held in its black silk scarf
Gone under the archway, home, he can join
The men that lounge in a group on the wharf.

His evening is a flame of wine
Among the eager, cordial men.
And she with her women hot and hard
Moves at her ease again.

> She is marked, she is singled out
>> For the fire:
> The brand is upon him, look you!
>> Of desire.

> They are chosen, ah, they are fated
>> For the fight!
> Champion her, all you women! Men, menfolk,
>> Hold him your light!

> Nourish her, train her, harden her,
>> Women all!
> Fold him, be good to him, cherish him,
>> Men, ere he fall.

> Women, another champion!
>> This, men, is yours!
> Wreathe and enlap and anoint them
>> Behind separate doors.

Gargnano.

Giorno dei Morti

Along the avenue of cypresses,
All in their scarlet cloaks and surplices
Of linen, go the chanting choristers,
The priests in gold and black, the villagers. . . .

And all along the path to the cemetery
The round dark heads of men crowd silently,
And black-scarved faces of womenfolk, wistfully
Watch at the banner of death, and the mystery.

And at the foot of a grave a father stands
With sunken head; and forgotten, folded hands;
And at the foot of a grave a mother kneels
With pale shut face, nor either hears nor feels

The coming of the chanting choristers
Between the avenue of cypresses,
The silence of the many villagers,
The candle-flames beside the surplices.

Loggerheads

Please yourself how you have it.
Take my words, and fling
Them down on the counter roundly;
See if they ring.

Sift my looks and expressions,
And see what proportion there is
Of sand in my doubtful sugar
Of verities.

Have a real stock-taking
Of my manly breast;
Find out if I'm sound or bankrupt,
Or a poor thing at best.

For I am quite indifferent
To your dubious state,
As to whether you've found a fortune
In me, or a flea-bitten fate.

Make a good investigation
Of all that is there,
And then, if it's worth it, be grateful—
If not, then despair.

If despair is our portion
Then let us despair.
Let us make for the weeping willow.
I don't care.

Coming Awake

When I woke, the lake-lights were quivering on the wall,
   The sunshine swam in a shoal across and across,
And a hairy, big bee hung over the primulas
   In the window, his body black fur, and the sound of him cross.

There was something I ought to remember: and yet
    I did not remember. Why should I? The running lights
And the airy primulas, oblivious
    Of the impending bee—they were fair enough sights.

People

The great gold apples of night
Hang from the street's long bough
    Dripping their light
On the faces that drift below,
On the faces that drift and blow
Down the night-time, out of sight
    In the wind's sad sough.

The ripeness of these apples of night
Distilling over me
    Makes sickening the white
Ghost-flux of faces that hie
Them endlessly, endlessly by
Without meaning or reason why
    They ever should be.

Peace

Peace is written on the doorstep
In lava.

Peace, black peace congealed.
My heart will know no peace
Till the hill bursts.

Brilliant, intolerable lava,
Brilliant as a powerful burning-glass,
Walking like a royal snake down the mountain towards the sea.

Forests, cities, bridges
Gone again in the bright trail of lava.
Naxos thousands of feet below the olive-roots,
And now the olive leaves thousands of feet below the lava fire.

Peace congealed in black lava on the doorstep.
Within, white-hot lava, never at peace
Till it burst forth blinding, withering the earth;
To set again into rock,
Grey-black rock.

Call it Peace?

Taormina.

From

Hibiscus and Salvia Flowers

Hark! Hark!
The dogs do bark!
It's the socialists come to town,
None in rags and none in tags,
Swaggering up and down.

Sunday morning,
And from the Sicilian townlets skirting Etna
The socialists have gathered upon us, to look at us.

How shall we know them when we see them?
How shall we know them now they've come?

43

Not by their rags and not by their tags,
Nor by any distinctive gown;
The same unremarkable Sunday suit
And hats cocked up and down.

Yet there they are, youths, loutishly
Strolling in gangs and staring along the Corso
With the gang-stare
And a half-threatening envy
At every *forestière*,
Every lordly tuppenny foreigner from the hotels, fattening on the
    exchange.

Hark! Hark!
The dogs do bark!
It's the socialists in the town.

Sans rags, sans tags,
Sans beards, sans bags,
Sans any distinction at all except loutish commonness.

How do we know then, that they are they?
Bolshevists.
Leninists.
Communists.
Socialists.
–Ists! –Ists!

Alas, salvia and hibiscus flowers.
Salvia and hibiscus flowers.

Listen again.
Salvia and hibiscus flowers.
Is it not so?
Salvia and hibiscus flowers.

Hark! Hark!
The dogs do bark!
Salvia and hibiscus flowers.

Who smeared their doors with blood?
Who on their breasts
Put salvias and hibiscus

Rosy, rosy scarlet.
And flame-rage, golden-throated
Bloom along the Corso on the living, perambulating bush.

Who said they might assume these blossoms?
What god did they consult?

Rose-red, princess hibiscus, rolling her pointed Chinese petals!
Azalea and camellia, single peony
And pomegranate bloom and scarlet mallow-flower
And all the eastern, exquisite royal plants
That noble blood has brought us down the ages!
Gently nurtured, frail and splendid
Hibiscus flower—
Alas, the Sunday coats of Sicilian bolshevists!

Pure blood, and noble blood, in the fine and rose-red veins;
Small, interspersed with jewels of white gold
Frail-filigreed among the rest;
Rose of the oldest races of princesses, Polynesian
Hibiscus.

Eve, in her happy moments,
Put hibiscus in her hair,
Before she humbled herself, and knocked her knees with repentance.

Sicilian bolshevists,
With hibiscus flowers in the buttonholes of your Sunday suits,
Come now, speaking of rights, what right have you to this flower?

The exquisite and ageless aristocracy
Of a peerless soul,
Blessed are the pure in heart and the fathomless in bright pride;
The loveliness that knows *noblesse oblige*;
The native royalty of red hibiscus flowers;
The exquisite assertion of new delicate life
Risen from the roots:
Is this how you'll have it, red-decked socialists,
Hibiscus-breasted?
If it be so, I fly to join you,
And if it be not so, brutes to pull down hibiscus flowers!

Taormina.

The Mosquito

When did you start your tricks,
Monsieur?

What do you stand on such high legs for?
Why this length of shredded shank,
You exaltation?

Is it so that you shall lift your centre of gravity upwards
And weigh no more than air as you alight upon me,
Stand upon me weightless, you phantom?

I heard a woman call you the Winged Victory
In sluggish Venice.
You turn your head towards your tail, and smile.

How can you put so much devilry
Into that translucent phantom shred
Of a frail corpus?

46

Queer, with your thin wings and your streaming legs,
How you sail like a heron, or a dull clot of air,
A nothingness.

Yet what an aura surrounds you;
Your evil little aura, prowling, and casting numbness on my mind.
That is your trick, your bit of filthy magic:
Invisibility, and the anæsthetic power
To deaden my attention in your direction.

But I know your game now, streaky sorcerer.
Queer, how you stalk and prowl the air
In circles and evasions, enveloping me,
Ghoul on wings
Winged Victory.

Settle, and stand on long thin shanks
Eyeing me sideways, and cunningly conscious that I am aware,
You speck.

I hate the way you lurch off sideways into the air
Having read my thoughts against you.

Come then, let us play at unawares,
And see who wins in this sly game of bluff.
Man or mosquito.

You don't know that I exist, and I don't know that you exist.
Now then!

It is your trump,
It is your hateful little trump,
You pointed fiend,
Which shakes my sudden blood to hatred of you:
It is your small, high, hateful bugle in my ear.

Why do you do it?
Surely it is bad policy.
They say you can't help it.

If that is so, then I believe a little in Providence protecting the
    innocent.
But it sounds so amazingly like a slogan,
A yell of triumph as you snatch my scalp.

Blood, red blood
Super-magical
Forbidden liquor.

I behold you stand
For a second enspasmed in oblivion,
Obscenely ecstasied
Sucking live blood,
My blood.

Such silence, such suspended transport,
Such gorging,
Such obscenity of trespass.

You stagger
As well as you may.
Only your accursed hairy frailty,
Your own imponderable weightlessness
Saves you, wafts you away on the very draught my anger makes
    in its snatching.

Away with a pæan of derision,
You winged blood-drop.

Can I not overtake you?
Are you one too many for me,
Winged Victory?
Am I not mosquito enough to out-mosquito you?

Queer what a big stain my sucked blood makes
Beside the infinitesimal faint smear of you!
Queer, what a dim dark smudge you have disappeared into!

Siracusa.

Bat

At evening, sitting on this terrace,
When the sun from the west, beyond Pisa, beyond the mountains
    of Carrara
Departs, and the world is taken by surprise . . .

When the tired flower of Florence is in gloom beneath the glowing
Brown hills surrounding . . .
When under the arches of the Ponte Vecchio
A green light enters against stream, flush from the west,
Against the current of obscure Arno . . .

Look up, and you see things flying
Between the day and the night;
Swallows with spools of dark thread sewing the shadows together.

A circle swoop, and a quick parabola under the bridge arches
Where light pushes through;
A sudden turning upon itself of a thing in the air.
A dip to the water.

And you think:
"The swallows are flying so late!"

Swallows?

49

Dark air-life looping
Yet missing the pure loop . . .
A twitch, a twitter, an elastic shudder in flight
And serrated wings against the sky,
Like a glove, a black glove thrown up at the light,
And falling back.

Never swallows!
Bats!
The swallows are gone.

At a wavering instant the swallows give way to bats
By the Ponte Vecchio . . .
Changing guard.

Bats, and an uneasy creeping in one's scalp
As the bats swoop overhead!
Flying madly.

Pipistrello!
Black piper on an infinitesimal pipe.
Little lumps that fly in air and have voices indefinite, wildly
vindictive;

Wings like bits of umbrella.

Bats!

Creatures that hang themselves up like an old rag, to sleep;
And disgustingly upside down.
Hanging upside down like rows of disgusting old rags
And grinning in their sleep.
Bats!

In China the bat is symbol of happiness.

Not for me!

Snake

A snake came to my water-trough
On a hot, hot day, and I in pyjamas for the heat,
To drink there.

In the deep, strange-scented shade of the great dark carob-tree
I came down the steps with my pitcher
And must wait, must stand and wait, for there he was at the trough
      before me.

He reached down from a fissure in the earth-wall in the gloom
And trailed his yellow-brown slackness soft-bellied down, over the
      edge of the stone trough
And rested his throat upon the stone bottom,
And where the water had dripped from the tap, in a small clearness,
He sipped with his straight mouth,
Softly drank through his straight gums, into his slack long body,
Silently.

Someone was before me at my water-trough,
And I, like a second comer, waiting.

He lifted his head from his drinking, as cattle do,
And looked at me vaguely, as drinking cattle do,
And flickered his two-forked tongue from his lips, and mused a
      moment,
And stooped and drank a little more,
Being earth-brown, earth-golden from the burning bowels of the
      earth
On the day of Sicilian July, with Etna smoking.

The voice of my education said to me
He must be killed,
For in Sicily the black, black snakes are innocent, the gold are
    venomous.

And voices in me said, If you were a man
You would take a stick and break him now, and finish him off.

But must I confess how I liked him,
How glad I was he had come like a guest in quiet, to drink at my
    water-trough
And depart peaceful, pacified, and thankless,
Into the burning bowels of this earth?

Was it cowardice, that I dared not kill him?
Was it perversity, that I longed to talk to him?
Was it humility, to feel so honoured?
I felt so honoured.

And yet those voices:
If you were not afraid, you would kill him!

And truly I was afraid, I was most afraid,
But even so, honoured still more
That he should seek my hospitality
From out the dark door of the secret earth.

He drank enough
And lifted his head, dreamily, as one who has drunken,
And flickered his tongue like a forked night on the air, so black;
Seeming to lick his lips,
And looked around like a god, unseeing, into the air,
And slowly turned his head,
And slowly, very slowly, as if thrice adream,
Proceeded to draw his slow length curving round
And climb again the broken bank of my wall-face.

And as he put his head into that dreadful hole,
And as he slowly drew up, snake-easing his shoulders, and entered
  farther,
A sort of horror, a sort of protest against his withdrawing into
  that horrid black hole,
Deliberately going into the blackness, and slowly drawing himself
  after,
Overcame me now his back was turned.

I looked round, I put down my pitcher,
I picked up a clumsy log
And threw it at the water-trough with a clatter.

I think it did not hit him,
But suddenly that part of him that was left behind convulsed in
  undignified haste,
Writhed like lightning, and was gone
Into the black hole, the earth-lipped fissure in the wall-front,
At which, in the intense still noon, I stared with fascination.

And immediately I regretted it.
I thought how paltry, how vulgar, what a mean act!
I despised myself and the voices of my accursed human education.

And I thought of the albatross,
And I wished he would come back, my snake.

For he seemed to me again like a king,
Like a king in exile, uncrowned in the underworld,
Now due to be crowned again.

And so, I missed my chance with one of the lords
Of life.
And I have something to expiate;
A pettiness.

Taormina.

53

Tortoise Family Connections

On he goes, the little one,
Bud of the universe,
Pediment of life.

Setting off somewhere, apparently.
Whither away, brisk egg?

His mother deposited him on the soil as if he were no more than
    droppings,
And now he scuffles tinily past her as if she were an old rusty tin.

A mere obstacle,
He veers round the slow great mound of her—
Tortoises always forsee obstacles.

It is no use my saying to him in an emotional voice:
"This is your Mother, she laid you when you were an egg."

He does not even trouble to answer: "Woman, what have I to
    do with thee?"
He wearily looks the other way,
And she even more wearily looks another way still,
Each with the utmost apathy,
Incognisant,
Unaware,
Nothing.

As for papa,
He snaps when I offer him his offspring,
Just as he snaps when I poke a bit of stick at him,
Because he is irascible this morning, an irascible tortoise
Being touched with love, and devoid of fatherliness.

Father and mother,
And three little brothers,
And all rambling aimless, like little perambulating pebbles scattered
    in the garden,
Not knowing each other from bits of earth or old tins.

Except that papa and mama are old acquaintances, of course,
Though family feeling there is none, not even the beginnings.
Fatherless, motherless, brotherless, sisterless
Little tortoise.

Row on then, small pebble,
Over the clods of the autumn, wind-chilled sunshine,
Young gaiety.

Does he look for a companion?

No, no, don't think it.
He doesn't know he is alone;
Isolation is his birthright,
This atom.

To row forward, and reach himself tall on spiny toes,
To travel, to burrow into a little loose earth, afraid of the night,
To crop a little substance,
To move, and to be quite sure that he is moving:
Basta!
To be a tortoise!
Think of it, in a garden of inert clods
A brisk, brindled little tortoise, all to himself—
Adam!

In a garden of pebbles and insects
To roam, and feel the slow heart beat
Tortoise-wise, the first bell sounding
From the warm blood, in the dark-creation morning.

Moving, and being himself,
Slow, and unquestioned,
And inordinately there, O stoic!
Wandering in the slow triumph of his own existence,
Ringing the soundless bell of his presence in chaos,
And biting the frail grass arrogantly,
Decidedly arrogantly.

Humming-Bird

I can imagine, in some other world
Primeval-dumb, far back
In that most awful stillness, that only gasped and hummed,
Humming-birds raced down the avenues.

Before anything had a soul,
While life was a heave of Matter, half inanimate,
This little bit chipped off in brilliance
And went whizzing through the slow, vast, succulent stems.

I believe there were no flowers then,
In the world where the humming-bird flashed ahead of creation.
I believe he pierced the slow vegetable veins with his long beak.

Probably he was big
As mosses, and little lizards, they say, were once big.
Probably he was jabbing, terrifying monster.

We look at him through the wrong end of the long telescope
     of Time,
Luckily for us.

Española.

Eagle in New Mexico

Towards the sun, towards the south-west
A scorched breast.
A scorched breast, breasting the sun like an answer,
Like a retort.

An eagle at the top of a low cedar-bush
On the sage-ash desert
Reflecting the scorch of the sun from his breast;
Eagle, with the sickle dripping darkly above.

Erect, scorched-pallid out of the hair of the cedar,
Erect, with the god-thrust entering him from below,
Eagle gloved in feathers
In scorched white feathers
In burnt dark feathers
In feathers still fire-rusted;
Sickle-overswept, sickle dripping over and above.

Sun-breaster,
Staring two ways at once, to right and left;
Masked-one
Dark-visaged
Sickle-masked
With iron between your two eyes;
You feather-gloved
To the feet;
Foot-fierce;
Erect one;
The god-thrust entering you steadily from below.

You never look at the sun with your two eyes.
Only the inner eye of your scorched broad breast
Looks straight at the sun.

You are dark
Except scorch-pale-breasted;
And dark cleaves down and weapon-hard downward curving
At your scorched breast,
Like a sword of Damocles,
Beaked eagle.

You've dipped it in blood so many times
That dark face-weapon, to temper it well,
Blood-thirsty bird.

Why do you front the sun so obstinately,
American eagle?
As if you owed him an old, old grudge, great sun: or an old, old
allegiance.

When you pick the red smoky heart from a rabbit or a light-
blooded bird
Do you lift it to the sun, as the Aztec priests used to lift red hearts
of men?

Does the sun need steam of blood do you think
In America, still,
Old eagle?

Does the sun in New Mexico sail like a fiery bird of prey in the
sky
Hovering?

Does he shriek for blood?
Does he fan great wings above the prairie, like a hovering, blood-
thirsty bird?

And are you his priest, big eagle
Whom the Indians aspire to?
Is there a bond of bloodshed between you?

Is your continent cold from the ice-age still, that the sun is so
     angry?
Is the blood of your continent somewhat reptilian still,
That the sun should be greedy for it?

I don't yield to you, big, jowl-faced eagle.
Nor you nor your blood-thirsty sun
That sucks up blood
Leaving a nervous people.

Fly off, big bird with a big black back.
Fly slowly away, with a rust of fire in your tail,
Dark as you are on your dark side, eagle of heaven.

Even the sun in heaven can be curbed and chastened at last
By the life in the hearts of men.
And you, great bird, sun-starer, heavy black beak
Can be put out of office as sacrifice bringer.

                                                    Taos.

The Blue Jay

The blue jay with a crest on his head
Comes round the cabin in the snow.
He runs in the snow like a bit of blue metal,
Turning his back on everything.

From the pine-tree that towers and hisses like a pillar of shaggy
     cloud
Immense above the cabin
Comes a strident laugh as we approach, this little black dog and I.
So halts the little black bitch on four spread paws in the snow

And looks up inquiringly into the pillar of cloud,
With a tinge of misgiving.
Ca-a-a! comes the scrape of ridicule out of the tree.

What voice of the Lord is that, from the tree of smoke?

Oh, Bibbles, little black bitch in the snow,
With a pinch of snow in the groove of your silly snub nose,
What do you look at *me* for?
What do you look at me for, with such misgiving?

It's the blue jay laughing at us.
It's the blue jay jeering at us, Bibs.

Every day since the snow is here
The blue jay paces round the cabin, very busy, picking up bits,
Turning his back on us all,
And bobbing his thick dark crest about the snow, as if darkly
    saying:
I ignore those folk who look out.

You acid-blue metallic bird,
You thick bird with a strong crest,
Who are you?
Whose boss are you, with all your bully way?
You copper-sulphate blue bird!

                                                                Lobo.

Kangaroo

In the northern hemisphere
Life seems to leap at the air, or skim under the wind
Like stags on rocky ground, or pawing horses, or springy scut-
    tailed rabbits.

Or else rush horizontal to charge at the sky's horizon,
Like bulls or bisons or wild pigs.

Or slip like water slippery towards its ends,
As foxes, stoats, and wolves, and prairie dogs.

Only mice, and moles, and rats, and badgers, and beavers, and
    perhaps bears
Seem belly-plumbed to the earth's mid-navel.
Or frogs that when they leap come flop, and flop to the centre
    of the earth.

But the yellow antipodal Kangaroo, when she sits up,
Who can unseat her, like a liquid drop that is heavy, and just
    touches earth.

The downward drip
The down-urge.
So much denser than cold-blooded frogs.

Delicate mother Kangaroo
Sitting up there rabbit-wise, but huge, plumb-weighted,
And lifting her beautiful slender face, oh! so much more gently
    and finely lined than a rabbit's, or than a hare's,
Lifting her face to nibble at a round white peppermint drop which
    she loves, sensitive mother Kangaroo.

Her sensitive, long, pure-bred face.
Her full antipodal eyes, so dark,
So big and quiet and remote, having watched so many empty
    dawns in silent Australia.

Her little loose hands, and drooping Victorian shoulders.
And then her great weight below the waist, her vast pale belly
With a thin young yellow little paw hanging out, and straggle
    of a long thin ear, like ribbon,
Like a funny trimming to the middle of her belly, thin little dangle
    of an immature paw, and one thin ear.

Her belly, her big haunches
And, in addition, the great muscular python-stretch of her tail.

There, she shan't have any more peppermint drops.
So she wistfully, sensitively sniffs the air, and then turns, goes off
in slow sad leaps

On the long flat skis of her legs,
Steered and propelled by that steel-strong snake of a tail.

Stops again, half turns, inquisitive to look back.
While something stirs quickly in her belly, and a lean little face
comes out, as from a window,
Peaked and a bit dismayed,
Only to disappear again quickly away from the sight of the world,
to snuggle down in the warmth,
Leaving the trail of a different paw hanging out.

Still she watches with eternal, cocked wistfulness!
How full her eyes are, like the full, fathomless, shining eyes of an
Australian black-boy
Who has been lost so many centuries on the margins of existence!

She watches with insatiable wistfulness.
Untold centuries of watching for something to come,
For a new signal from life, in that silent lost land of the South.

Where nothing bites but insects and snakes and the sun, small life.
Where no bull roared, no cow ever lowed, no stag cried, no
leopard screeched, no lion coughed, no dog barked,
But all was silent save for parrots occasionally, in the haunted
blue bush.

Wistfully watching, with wonderful liquid eyes.
And all her weight, all her blood, dripping sack-wise down
    towards the earth's centre,
And the live little-one taking in its paw at the door of her belly.

Leap then, and come down on the line that draws to the earth's
    deep, heavy centre.

Sydney.

Elephants in the Circus

Elephants in the circus
have æons of weariness round their eyes.
Yet they sit up
and show vast bellies to the children.

Two Performing Elephants

He stands with his forefeet on the drum
and the other, the old one, the pallid hoary female
must creep her great bulk beneath the bridge of him.

On her knees, in utmost caution
all agog, and curling up her trunk
she edges through without upsetting him.
Triumph! the ancient, pig-tailed monster!

When her trick is to climb over him
with what shadow-like slow carefulness
she skims him, sensitive
as shadows from the ages gone and perished
in touching him, and planting her round feet.

While the wispy, modern children, half-afraid
watch silent. The looming of the hoary, far-gone ages
is too much for them.

Destiny

O destiny, destiny,
do you exist, and can a man touch your hand?
O destiny
if I could see your hand, and it were thumbs down,
I would be willing to give way, like the pterodactyl,
and accept obliteration.
I would not even ask to leave a fossil claw extant,
nor a thumb-mark like a clue,
I would be willing to vanish completely, completely.

But if it is thumbs up, and mankind must go on being mankind,
then I am willing to fight, I will roll my sleeves up
and start in.

Only, O destiny
I wish you'd show your hand.

A Living

A man should never earn his living,
if he earns his life he'll be lovely.

A bird
picks up its seeds or little snails
between heedless earth and heaven
in heedlessness.

But, the plucky little sport, it gives to life
song, and chirruping, gay feathers, fluff-shadowed warmth
and all the unspeakable charm of birds hopping and fluttering and
    being birds.
—And we, we get it all from them for nothing.

Things Men Have Made—

Things men have made with wakened hands, and put soft life into
are awake through years with transferred touch, and go on glowing
for long years.
And for this reason, some old things are lovely
warm still with the life of forgotten men who made them.

Let Us Be Men—

For God's sake, let us be men
not monkeys minding machines
or sitting with our tails curled
while the machine amuses us, the radio or film or gramophone.

Monkeys with a bland grin on our faces.—

What is He?

What is he?
—A man, of course.
Yes, but what does he do?
—He lives and is a man.

Oh quite! but he must work. He must have a job of some sort.
—Why?
Because obviously he's not one of the leisured classes.
—I don't know. He has lots of leisure. And he makes quite beautiful
    chairs.—
There you are then! He's a cabinet maker.
—No no!
Anyhow a carpenter and joiner.
—Not at all.
But you said so.
—What did I say?
That he made chairs, and was a joiner and carpenter.
—I said he made chairs, but I did not say he was a carpenter.
All right then, he's just an amateur.
—Perhaps! Would you say a thrush was a professional flautist,
    or just an amateur?—
I'd say it was just a bird.
—And I say he is just a man.
All right! You always did quibble.

Spray

It is a wonder foam is so beautiful.
A wave bursts in anger on a rock, broken up
in wild white sibilant spray
and falls back, drawing in its breath with rage,
with frustration how beautiful!

66

Sea-Weed

Sea-weed sways and sways and swirls
as if swaying were its form of stillness;
and if it flushes against fierce rock
it slips over it as shadows do, without hurting itself.

Many Mansions

When a bird flips his tail in getting his balance on a tree
he feels much gayer than if somebody had left him a fortune
or than if he'd just built himself a nest with a bathroom—
Why can't people be gay like that?

Poverty

The only people I ever heard talk about My Lady Poverty
were rich people, or people who imagined themselves rich.
Saint Francis himself was a rich and spoiled young man.

Being born among the working people
I know that poverty is a hard old hag,
and a monster, when you're pinched for actual necessities.
And whoever says she isn't, is a liar.

I don't want to be poor, it means I am pinched.
But neither do I want to be rich.
When I look at this pine-tree near the sea,
that grows out of rock, and plumes forth, plumes forth,
I see it has a natural abundance.

With its roots it has a grand grip on its daily bread,
and its plumes look like green cups held up to the sun and air
and full of wine.

I want to be like that, to have a natural abundance
and plume forth, and be splendid.

Talk

I wish people, when you sit near them,
wouldn't think it necessary to make conversation
and send thin draughts of words
blowing down your neck and your ears
and giving you a cold in your inside.

Can't Be Borne

Any woman who says to me
—Do you really love me?—
earns my undying detestation.

After All the Tragedies Are Over—

After all the tragedies are over and worn out
and a man can no longer feel heroic about being a Hamlet—
When love is gone, and desire is dead, and tragedy has left the
heart
then grief and pain go too, withdrawing
from the heart and leaving strange cold stretches of sand.

So a man no longer knows his own heart;
he might say into the twilight: What is it?
I am here, yet my heart is bare and utterly empty.
I have passed from existence, I feel nothing any more.
I am a nonentity.—

Yet, when the time has come to be nothing, how good it is to be
    nothing!
a waste expanse of nothing, like wide foreshores where not a
    ripple is left
and the sea is lost
in the lapse of the lowest of tides.

Ah, when I have seen myself left by life, left nothing!

Yet even waste, grey foreshores, sand, and sorry, far-out clay
are sea-bed still, through their hour of bare denuding
It is the moon that turns the tides.
The beaches can do nothing about it.

The Optimist

    The optimist builds himself safe inside a cell
    and paints the inside walls sky-blue
    and blocks up the door
    and says he's in heaven.

Lizard

A lizard ran out on a rock and looked up, listening
no doubt to the sounding of the spheres.
And what a dandy fellow! the right toss of a chin for you
and swirl of a tail!

If men were as much men as lizards are lizards
they'd be worth looking at.

Censors

Censors are dead men
set up to judge between life and death.
For no live, sunny man would be a censor,
he'd just laugh.

But censors, being dead men,
have a stern eye on life.
—That thing's alive! It's dangerous. Make away
        with it!—
And when the execution is performed
you hear the stertorous, self-righteous heavy
        breathing of the dead men,
the censors, breathing with relief.

Now It's Happened

One cannot now help thinking
how much better it would have been
if Vronsky and Anna Karenin
had stood up for themselves, and seen

Russia across her crisis,
instead of leaving it to Lenin.

The big, flamboyant Russia
might have been saved, if a pair
of rebels like Anna and Vronsky
had blasted the sickly air
of Dostoevsky and Tchekov,
and spy-government everywhere.

But Tolstoi was a traitor
to the Russia that needed him most,
the clumsy, bewildered Russia
so worried by the Holy Ghost.
He shifted his job on to the peasants
and landed them all on toast.

Dostoevsky, the Judas,
with his sham christianity
epileptically ruined
the last bit of sanity
left in the hefty bodies
of the Russian nobility.

So our goody-good men betray us
and our sainty-saints let us down,
and a sickly people will slay us
if we touch the sob-stuff crown
of such martyrs; while Marxian tenets
naturally take hold of the town.

Too much of the humble Willy wet-leg
and the holy can't-help-it touch,
till you've ruined a nation's fibre
and they loathe all feeling as such,
and want to be cold and devilish hard
like machines—and you can't wonder much.—

Intimates

Don't you care for my love? she said bitterly.

I handed her the mirror, and said:
Please address these questions to the proper person!
Please make all requests to head-quarters!
In all matters of emotional importance
please approach the supreme authority direct!—
So I handed her the mirror.

And she would have broken it over my head,
but she caught sight of her own reflection
and that held her spellbound for two seconds
while I fled.

Trees in the Garden

Ah in the thunder air
how still the trees are!

And the lime-tree, lovely and tall, every leaf silent
hardly looses even a last breath of perfume.

And the ghostly, creamy coloured little trees of leaves
white, ivory white among the rambling greens
how evanescent, variegated elder, she hesitates on the green grass
as if, in another moment, she would disappear
with all her grace of foam!

And the larch that is only a column, it goes up too tall to see:
And the balsam-pines that are blue with the grey-blue blueness of
    things from the sea,
And the young copper beech, its leaves red-rosy at the ends
how still they are together, they stand so still
in the thunder air, all strangers to one another
as the green grass glows upwards, strangers in the garden.

Lichtental.

The Greeks Are Coming!

Little islands out at sea, on the horizon
keep suddenly showing a whiteness, a flash and a furl, a hail
of something coming, ships a-sail from over the rim of the sea.

And every time, it is ships, it is ships,
it is ships of Cnossos coming, out of the morning end of the sea,
it is Aegean ships, and men with archaic pointed beards
coming out of the eastern end.

But it is far-off foam.
And an ocean liner, going east, like a small bettle walking the edge
is leaving a long thread of dark smoke
like a bad smell.

The Argonauts

They are not dead, they are not dead!
Now that the sun, like a lion, licks his paws
and goes slowly down the hill:

now that the moon, who remembers, and only cares
that we should be lovely in the flesh, with bright, crescent feet,
pauses near the crest of the hill, climbing slowly, like a queen
looking down on the lion as he retreats—

Now the sea is the Argonauts' sea, and in the dawn
Odysseus calls the commands, as he steers past those foamy islands;
wait, wait, don't bring the coffee yet, nor the *pain grillé*.
The dawn is not off the sea, and Odysseus' ships
have not yet passed the islands, I must watch them still.

Middle of the World

This sea will never die, neither will it ever grow old
nor cease to be blue, nor in the dawn
cease to lift up its hills
and let the slim black ship of Dionysos come sailing in
with grape-vines up the mast, and dolphins leaping.

What do I care if the smoking ships
of the P. & O. and the Orient Line and all the other stinkers
cross like clock-work the Minoan distance!
They only cross, the distance never changes.

And now that the moon who gives men glistening bodies
is in her exaltation, and can look down on the sun
I see descending from the ships at dawn
slim naked men from Cnossos, smiling the archaic smile
of those that will without fail come back again,
and kindling little fires upon the shores
and crouching, and speaking the music of lost languages.

And the Minoan Gods, and the Gods of Tiryns
are heard softly laughing and chatting, as ever;
and Dionysos, young, and a stranger
leans listening on the gate, in all respect.

They Say the Sea is Loveless

They say the sea is loveless, that in the sea
love cannot live, but only bare, salt splinters
of loveless life.

But from the sea
the dolphins leap round Dionysos' ship
whose masts have purple vines,
and up they come with the purple dark of rainbows
and flip! they go! with the nose-dive of sheer delight;
and the sea is making love to Dionysos
in the bouncing of these small and happy whales.

Butterfly

Butterfly, the wind blows sea-ward, strong beyond the garden wall!
Butterfly, why do you settle on my shoe, and sip the dirt on my shoe,
Lifting your veined wings, lifting them? big white butterfly!

Already it is October, and the wind blows strong to the sea
from the hills where snow must have fallen, the wind is polished
     with snow.
Here in the garden, with red geraniums, it is warm, it is warm
but the wind blows strong to sea-ward, white butterfly, content on
     my shoe!

Will you go, will you go from my warm house?
Will you climb on your big soft wings, black-dotted,
as up an invisible rainbow, an arch
till the wind slides you sheer from the arch-crest
and in a strange level fluttering you go out to sea-ward, white speck!

Farewell, farewell, lost soul!
you have melted in the crystalline distance,
it is enough! I saw you vanish into air.

Bavarian Gentians

Not every man has gentians in his house
in Soft September, at slow, sad Michaelmas.

Bavarian gentians, big and dark, only dark
darkening the day-time, torch-like with the smoking blueness of
    Pluto's gloom,
ribbed and torch-like, with their blaze of darkness spread blue
down flattening into points, flattened under the sweep of white day
torch-flower of the blue-smoking darkness, Pluto's dark-blue daze,
black lamps from the halls of Dis, burning dark blue,
giving off darkness, blue darkness, as Demeter's pale lamps give off
    light,
lead me then, lead the way.

Reach me a gentian, give me a torch!
let me guide myself with the blue, forked torch of this flower
down the darker and darker stairs, where blue is darkened on blue-
    ness
even where Persephone goes, just now, from the frosted September
to the sightless realm where darkness is awake upon the dark
and Persephone herself is but a voice

or a darkness invisible enfolded in the deeper dark
of the arms Plutonic, and pierced with the passion of dense gloom,
among the splendour of torches of darkness, shedding darkness on
   the lost bride and her groom.

In the Cities

In the cities
there is even no more any weather
the weather in town is always benzine, or else petrol fumes
lubricating oil, exhaust gas.

As over some dense marsh, the fumes
thicken, miasma, the fumes of the automobile
densely thicken in the cities.

In ancient Rome, down the thronged streets
no wheels might run, no insolent chariots.
Only the footsteps, footsteps
of people
and the gentle trotting of the litter-bearers.

In Minos, in Mycenae
in all the cities with lion gates
the dead threaded the air, lingering
lingering in the earth's shadow
and leaning towards the old hearth.

In London, New York, Paris
in the bursten cities
the dead tread heavily through the muddy air
through the mire of fumes
heavily, stepping weary on our hearts.

Mana of the Sea

Do you see the sea, breaking itself to bits against the islands
yet remaining unbroken, the level great sea?

Have I caught from it
the tide in my arms
that runs down to the shallows of my wrists, and breaks
abroad in my hands, like waves among the rocks of substance?

Do the rollers of the sea
roll down my thighs
and over the submerged islets of my knees
with power, sea-power
sea-power
to break against the ground
in the flat, recurrent breakers of my two feet?

And is my body ocean, ocean
whose power runs to the shores along my arms
and breaks in the foamy hands, whose power rolls out
to the white-treading waves of two salt feet?

I am the sea, I am the sea!

Mystic

They call all experience of the senses *mystic*, when the experience
    is considered.
So an apple becomes *mystic* when I taste in it
the summer and the snows, the wild welter of earth
and the insistence of the sun.

78

All of which things I can surely taste in a good apple.
Though some apples taste preponderantly of water, wet and sour
and some of too much sun, brackish sweet
like lagoon-water, that has been too much sunned.

If I say I taste these things in an apple, I am called *mystic*, which
      means a liar.
The only way to eat an apple is to hog it down like a pig
and taste nothing
that is *real*.

But if I eat an apple, I like to eat it with all my senses awake.
Hogging it down like a pig I call the feeding of corpses.

Anaxagoras

When Anaxagoras says: Even the snow is black!
he is taken by the scientists very seriously
because he is enunciating a "principle", a "law"
that all things are mixed, and therefore the purest white snow
has in it an element of blackness.

That they call science, and reality.
I call it mental conceit and mystification
and nonsense, for pure snow is white to us
white and white and only white
with a lovely bloom of whiteness upon white
in which the soul delights and the senses
have an experience of bliss.

And life is for delight, and for bliss
and dread, and the dark, rolling ominousness of doom
then the bright dawning of delight again
from off the sheer white snow, or the poised moon.

And in the shadow of the sun the snow is blue, so blue-aloof
with a hint of the frozen bells of the scylla flower
but never the ghost of a glimpse of Anaxagoras' funeral black.

Death is Not Evil, Evil is Mechanical

Only the human being, absolved from kissing and strife
goes on and on and on, without wandering
fixed upon the hub of the ego
going, yet never wandering, fixed, yet in motion,
the kind of hell that is real, grey and awful
sinless and stainless going round and round
the kind of hell grey Dante never saw
but of which he had a bit inside him.

Know thyself, and that thou art mortal.
But know thyself, denying that thou art mortal:
a thing of kisses and strife
a lit-up shaft of rain
a calling column of blood
a rose tree bronzey with thorns
a mixture of yea and nay
a rainbow of love and hate
a wind that blows back and forth
a creature of beautiful peace, like a river
and a creature of conflict, like a cataract:
know thyself, in denial of all these things—

And thou shalt begin to spin round on the hub of the obscene ego
a grey void thing that goes without wandering
a machine that in itself is nothing
a centre of the evil world.

The Ship of Death

I

Now it is autumn and the falling fruit
and the long journey towards oblivion.

The apples falling like great drops of dew
to bruise themselves an exit from themselves.

And it is time to go, to bid farewell
to one's own self, and find an exit
from the fallen self.

II

Have you built your ship of death, O have you?
O build your ship of death, for you will need it.

The grim frost is at hand, when the apples will fall
thick, almost thundrous, on the hardened earth.

And death is on the air like a smell of ashes!
Ah! can't you smell it?

And in the bruised body, the frightened soul
finds itself shrinking, wincing from the cold
that blows upon it through the orifices.

III

And can a man his own quietus make
with a bare bodkin?

With daggers, bodkins, bullets, man can make
a bruise or break of exit for his life;
but is that a quietus, O tell me, is it quietus?

Surely not so! for how could murder, even self-murder
ever a quietus make?

IV

O let us talk of quiet that we know,
that we can know, the deep and lovely quiet
of a strong heart at peace!

How can we this, our own quietus, make?

V

Build then the ship of death, for you must take
the longest journey, to oblivion.

And die the death, the long and painful death
that lies between the old self and the new.

Already our bodies are fallen, bruised, badly bruised,
already our souls are oozing through the exit
of the cruel bruise.

Already the dark and endless ocean of the end
is washing in through the breaches of our wounds,
already the flood is upon us.

Oh build your ship of death, your little ark
and furnish it with food, with little cakes, and wine
for the dark flight down oblivion.

VI

Piecemeal the body dies, and the timid soul
has her footing washed away, as the dark flood rises.

We are dying, we are dying, we are all of us dying
and nothing will stay the death-flood rising within us
and soon it will rise on the world, on the outside world.

We are dying, we are dying, piecemeal our bodies are dying
and our strength leaves us,
and our soul cowers naked in the dark rain over the flood,
cowering in the last branches of the tree of our life.

VII

We are dying, we are dying, so all we can do
is now to be willing to die, and to build the ship
of death to carry the soul on the longest journey.

A little ship, with oars and food
and little dishes, and all accoutrements
fitting and ready for the departing soul.

Now launch the small ship, now as the body dies
and life departs, launch out, the fragile soul
in the fragile ship of courage, the ark of faith
with its store of food and little cooking pans
and change of clothes,
upon the flood's black waste
upon the waters of the end
upon the sea of death, where still we sail
darkly, for we cannot steer, and have no port.

There is no port, there is nowhere to go
only the deepening blackness darkening still
blacker upon the soundless, ungurgling flood
darkness at one with darkness, up and down
and sideways utterly dark, so there is no direction any more.
and the little ship is there; yet she is gone.
She is not seen, for there is nothing to see her by.
She is gone! gone! and yet
somewhere she is there.
Nowhere!

VIII

And everything is gone, the body is gone
completely under, gone, entirely gone.
The upper darkness is heavy as the lower,
between them the little ship
is gone
she is gone.

It is the end, it is oblivion.

IX

And yet out of eternity, a thread
separates itself on the blackness,
a horizontal thread
that fumes a little with pallor upon the dark.

Is it illusion? or does the pallor fume
A little higher?
Ah wait, wait, for there's the dawn,
the cruel dawn of coming back to life
out of oblivion.

Wait, wait, the little ship
drifting, beneath the deathly ashy grey
of a flood-dawn.

Wait, wait! even so, a flush of yellow
and strangely, O chilled wan soul, a flush of rose.

A flush of rose, and the whole thing starts again.

X

The flood subsides, and the body, like a worn sea-shell
emerges strange and lovely.
And the little ship wings home, faltering and lapsing
on the pink flood.
and the frail soul steps out, into her house again
filling the heart with peace.

Swings the heart renewed with peace
even of oblivion.

Oh build your ship of death, oh build it!
for you will need it.
For the voyage of oblivion awaits you.

All Soul's Day

Be careful, then, and be gentle about death.
For it is hard to die, it is difficult to go through
the door, even when it opens.

And the poor dead, when they have left the walled
and silvery city of the now hopeless body
where are they to go, Oh where are they to go?

They linger in the shadow of the earth.
The earth's long conical shadow is full of souls
that cannot find the way across the sea of change.

Be kind, Oh be kind to your dead
and give them a little encouragement
and help them to build their little ship of death.

For the soul has a long, long journey after death
to the sweet home of pure oblivion.
Each needs a little ship, a little ship
and the proper store of meal for the longest journey.

Oh, from out of your heart
provide for your dead once more, equip them
like departing mariners, lovingly.

Shadows

And if tonight my soul may find her peace
in sleep, and sink in good oblivion,
and in the morning wake like a new-opened flower
then I have been dipped again in God, and new-created.
And if, as weeks go round, in the dark of the moon
my spirit darkens and goes out, and soft strange gloom
pervades my movements and my thoughts and words
then I shall know that I am walking still
with God, we are close together now the moon's in shadow.

And if, as autumn deepens and darkens
I feel the pain of falling leaves, and stems that break in storms
and trouble and dissolution and distress
and then the softness of deep shadows folding, folding
around my soul and spirit, around my lips
so sweet, like a swoon, or more like the drowse of a low, sad song
singing darker than the nightingale, on, on to the solstice
and the silence of short days, the silence of the year, the shadow,
then I shall know that my life is moving still
with the dark earth, and drenched
with the deep oblivion of earth's lapse and renewal.

And if, in the changing phases of man's life
I fall in sickness and in misery
my wrists seem broken and my heart seems dead
and strength is gone, and my life
is only the leavings of a life:

and still, among it all, snatches of lovely oblivion, and snatches of
    renewal
odd, wintry flowers upon the withered stem, yet new, strange
    flowers
such as my life has not brought forth before, new blossoms of me—

then I must know that still
I am in the hands [of] the unknown God,
he is breaking me down to his own oblivion
to send me forth on a new morning, a new man.

We Have Gone Too Far

We have gone too far, oh very much too far,
Only attend to the noiseless multitudes
Of ghosts that throng about our muffled hearts.

Only behold the ghosts, the ghosts of the slain,
Behold them homeless and houseless, without complaint
Of their patient waiting upon us, the throng of the ghosts.

And say, what matters any more, what matters,
Save the cold ghosts that homeless flock about
Our serried hearts, drifting without a place?

What matters any more, but only love?
There's only love that matters any more.
There's only love, the rest is all outspent.

Let us receive our ghosts and give them place,
Open the ranks, and let them in our hearts,
And lay them deep in love, lay them to sleep.

The foe can take our goods, our homes and land,
Also the lives that still he may require,
But leave us still to love, still leave us love.

Leave us to take our ghosts into our hearts,
To lap them round with love, and lay them by
To sleep at last in immemorial love.

We let the weapons slip from out our hands,
We loose our grip, and we unstrain our eyes,
We let our souls be pure and vulnerable.

We cover the houseless dead, so they sleep in peace,
We yield the enemy his last demands,
So he too may be healed, be soothed to peace.

For now the hosts of homeless ghosts do throng
To many about us, so we wander about
Blind with the gossamer of prevalent death.

But let us free our eyes, and look beyond
This serried ecstasy of prevalent death,
And pass beyond, with the foe and the homeless ghosts.

Let us rise up, and go from out this grey
Last twilight of the Gods, to find again
The lost Hesperides where love is pure.

For we have gone too far, oh much too far
Towards the darkness and the shadow of death;
Let us turn back, lest we should all be lost.

Let us go back now, though we give up all
The treasure and the vaunt we ever had,
Let us go back, the only way is love.

Beyond the Rockies

There are people there, beyond the Rockies
As there are people here, on this side.

But the people there, beyond the Rockies
Seem always to be asking, asking something.

The new moon sets at sundown,
And there, beyond the sunset, quivers.

An Indian, walking wrapt in his winding sheet
Answers the question as he puts it, in his stride.

Mexicans, like people who have died
Ask, in the space of their eyes:
What have we lost?

What have we lost, in the west?
We who have gone west?
There is no answer.

In the land of the lost
Nothing but to make lost music.

On the rim of the desert
Round the lost man's camp-fire
Watch the new moon
Curved, cut the last threads.

It is finished: the rest is afterwards
With grey on the floor of the desert,
And more space than in life.

INDEX OF TITLES AND FIRST LINES